WITH OUR BODIES WE NURSE OUR
MACHINE THAT KILLED US.

WE GIVE IT ALL OF OUR WORDS.

AHSAHTA PRESS

BOISE, IDAHO   2016

THE NEW SERIES #77

AFTER WE ALL DIED

Allison Cobb

Ahsahta Press, Boise State University, Boise, Idaho 83725-1525
Cover design by Quemadura / Book design by Janet Holmes
ahsahtapress.org

LIBRARY OF CONGRESS
CATALOGING-IN-PUBLICATION DATA

Names: Cobb, Allison, author.
Title: After we all died / Allison Cobb.
Description: Boise, Idaho : Ahsahta Press, 2016. | Series: The new series ;
 #77
Identifiers: LCCN 2016039058| ISBN 9781934103739 (pbk. : alk. paper) | ISBN
 193410373X (pbk. : alk. paper)
Classification: LCC PS3603.O225 A6 2016 | DDC 813/.6--DC23
LC record available at https://lccn.loc.gov/2016039058

ACKNOWLEDGMENTS

Poems and essays in this book first appeared in the following publications. I'm grateful
to the editors: "What the businessman said," Poem-a-Day, Academy of American Poets;
"The things you loved" and "For love," *Across the Margins,* ed. Richard Roundy; "Sing,"
"Sorry," "Poem called More," and "Moo," *Brooklyn Rail,* ed. Anselm Berrigan; "Poem
of Force," *Capitalism, Nature, Socialism,* ed. Jules Boykoff; "I forgive you," *Denver
Quarterly,* ed. Laird Hunt; "Ark," "Dear corporate," and "Sentences. August 6," *Dream
Salon,* ed. Chris Ashby; "I heart," *Dreamboat,* ed. Alli Warren; "I made this," *Elderly,*
eds. Nick DeBoer and Jamie Townsend; "Nature poem," *Picture Sentence,* eds. Robert
Tomlinson and Margaret Donsbach Tomlinson; "You were born," *Talisman,* ed. Lisa
Bourbeau; and "Drone poem," *Tripwire,* ed. David Buuck. "Look" appeared in the
anthology *Make It True: Poetry from Cascadia,* eds. Nadine Maestas, Barry McKinnon,
Paul Nelson and George Stanley

I'm grateful to Playa for a residency that sparked the writing of this book, and to the
Djerassi Resident Artists Program for helping enable its completion.

This book is dedicated to incurable and beautiful and awful Love, for which we die and
must be born, and to my loves, especially Jen Coleman, Sue Landers, and Paula Ward,
who nurtured the book and me.

Contents

AFTER WE ALL DIED

I forgive you fingers. I forgive you wrists and palms. I forgive you web
of veins, the nameless knuckles, twenty-seven bones, the nails and
moons below. I forgive you feet, the toes and toenails, metatarsals arch-
ing up, cuneiform, the cuboids, and navicular. I forgive you sole of foot,
fibrofatty pressure chambers, dense packed nerve and tissue, the spring
ligament. I forgive you ankle, lovely with twin bone swells. I forgive you
calf abundant, knee cap, knee joint extra complex and temperamental. I
forgive you bone and sinew, blood vessel and braid of muscle. I forgive
you tidal lymph. I forgive you skin, the coast on which all washes up. I
forgive you thigh and buttock, anus, vagina, clitoris, urethra, mons a
rounded mass of fatty tissue, inner and outer lips, the smooth stretch of
perineum. I forgive you sacroiliac, the bone wings laced with tendon, the
pelvic inlet and the brim. I forgive you coiled intestines lined in tissue
soft as velvet, the uterus and eggs inside of ovaries, the fluting tubes
Fallopian, the docile stomach sack. I forgive you my esophagus, moist
mucosa, heart and lung lobes, liver, kidneys, pancreas and gall bladder,
the spleen—all the inner organs curled together in the dark and mut-
tering like clocks, like memories of clocks. I forgive you. I forgive you
breasts, your lobes and lobules, ducts and alveoli rising to the darkened
areola and the nipple passage outward. I forgive you golden seams of fat
in semi-liquid state, encasing in your oily cells the poisons of the world.
I forgive you mouth, the teeth and budded tongue, the epiglottis, phar-
ynx and the tough-ringed trachea, the larynx with its cords for making
sound. I forgive you nasal cavity and sinuses, the ear canal and clear-
walled eyeballs—all the head holes opened to the rain of light, the

floating atoms of the air, the jacked together molecules of the stupid human world. I forgive you ropey muscles of the neck and face, so overstrained from constantly composing mirrors. I forgive you brain, three pounds of convoluted meat plastered with grey nerve cells, wrapped in blood-rich tissue, floating in your own sweet bath of fluid. I forgive you spinal column sprouting from the brain stem, flaring wires to spark electric charges through dumb tissue. I forgive you glands, both tubular and alveolar, releasing streams of chemicals and mucus, sweat and milk and oil. I forgive you every hair bulb, constantly dividing, pressing hardened protein shafts up toward the light. I forgive you cells, all one hundred trillion, the inner ocean that has ebbed and flowed across three million years. I forgive you every part performing all the intricate and simple tasks that make this mass alive. I forgive you all for already having died.

I.

SO IN LOVE

god we created
all without
form and void—a sea
of zombie *haute*
coo—here comes all
the flesh you ever ate
in living form with eyes
to look you back—to look
you god we chemists
in the face gleam
stitch the sickest thread
through every earth
-born body—Angel
Mounted monks display
their taxidermy—means
arrange the skin
for war—the single
tree of every
rose room weeping
birds—please
put us in your
book she said my
body sailing
past the factory
lights at night all

lives outside
this ark un
-branded sink

I made this

for Stephen Collis and Roy Scranton

I.

To get face to face
with death, we drive
over to the Build-a-Bear store—all
those flat skins with their
insertion holes. A thing there is
that wants a little warmth, the fur
curled on the thigh, the rat
making scratching sounds down
below, whatever
left bite marks all across
the baby, our lives
infused with
brand meaning—you know the feeling
you get from the Gap. Real shit
don't stick to that khaki, the history
of which is complex: The British
once wore blood red to battle,
but in the beige sands
of the Punjab they stuck out like
bull flags. Also, it was hot as hell.
So, the story goes, the colonial
recruits in Peshawar wore their
pajamas to war—totally

un-British, I know! But don't sneer,
they rubbed their cotton sleepwear
in dirt to disappear against the earth
they sought to conquer. It worked, the dye
of Empire bled through India
and down to the Boer War—and the West
got khaki, the fabric that says
"adventure." The word is Urdu
for—you know—dirty. *Kakka*, the ancient
proto-word word for shit. *Kaki?* my
Polish landlord in Brooklyn asked,
incredulous, when I showed him my
strung out upstairs neighbors pooped
on my fire escape. *Kaki* I replied
with that tone of total finality
reserved only for incidents
of human waste. We both knew
just what we meant. I got a text
from the City saying DON'T
DRINK THE WATER because of *e. coli*,
which thrives in the intestines. You are only a skin
bag for your microbiome,
my clown friend. Bacteria evolved
a human meat car
to get around in. Maybe

they wanted to move someplace
warm. Maybe they put in the minds
of the British a desire to conquer, a desire
for business casual attire. The house
held piles of mouse shit
in every drawer. I am very clean, sir,
I swear. A rat has made its domicile
inside my crawl space. I saw its scaly
tail slip in through a hole. I bet it has
a big family in there. I heard the trap
snap on its
little fur skull. Rats arrived
with the colonists about the year
the founding
fathers declared
their independence. *You are never*
more than twenty feet
from a rat, said some British
expert in some paper. We tried to forget
ours was down there. After a while
we could no longer ignore
the smell, so we eased our way
into the hole and saw
the rat with its smashed head very
dead but filled

with crawling things which made
Jen make a gagging sound
near my ear—*not*
helping, I told her. Rats don't
see well so they spray scent trails
out of urine and feces. Dragonflies
can see 360 degrees. I watched one
land on a garlic stalk in my yard, turning its
bulb-eyed head back and forth. Its eyes looked
fake, like formed from plastic or some
secret military-grade material. Scientists
stick probes inside the brains
and eyes of dragonflies to figure out
what makes them such good hunters. The CIA
supposedly made robot dragonfly
spy drones, but this one was real—
I could tell because I saw a thin
thread of yellowish waste drop out
the end of it. True. Like that book
says, *Everyone Poops,* even
Bridesmaids. What a movie. "See all
topics for *e. coli.*" I am not trying
to be gross. I was going somewhere
with this but then I got, um,
sick, and had to stay put

near the toilet. You know how it is,
mon clown, to have a crawl
space crawling right up
the middle
of your self. Doctors call it
the digestive tract. They consider it
outside you. It's the way you take
in the world, or more precise, the way the world
runs through you. Bacteria
patrol your borders, keeping out
the undesirables. Not for your sake, except—
as their house, food, and transport—they like
to keep you alive. Of course they do not
always succeed.

II.

The news report says the clown showed up
at the graveyard I once lived beside
in Brooklyn, same apartment as
the *kaki* incident. The clown wore
a string of pink
balloons around its neck, but not light,
they were heavy and pulled its red nose

right down to soil. People think
it's disrespectful. They say the clown left
behind a Build-a-Bear bag, a lady's
parasol and some Fritos. I think
it's performance art. Why shouldn't the dead
enjoy that as much
as we do? Seriously, Doctor
Theodor Escherich discovered
e. coli, which was named for him
after he died. He studied—true
story—the fæces of babies. You
know the saying—two things in life
come on quick: war
and diarrhea. It turns out that
setting up the trap is much easier
than dealing with the body. *Send in
the clowns* is what theatre people say
when they know the show's not
going well. Okay. I traveled to that graveyard
in my mind, near
Sylvan Lake where the Italians
built their fancy mausoleums. I like to think
of it—death—as the "great outdoors"
the clown told me, but not in
so many words. I like to think

of shit as the tenebrous edge between the living
and the dead, I said in return, like Darwin,
who spent a lot of time with his face
in the dirt and came back to report
that pretty much the whole surface
of earth had passed through
worm intestines. Like the lady
in Portland who doesn't use her
plumbing. She composts it all for
her garden. She handed me a pure white,
bulbous head of garlic and said
I made this. We all understood
the significance. Egyptians fed garlic
for strength to their pyramid-
building slaves. The pharaohs
also kept clowns at court "to rejoice
and delight the heart." I put on
the clown's pink flesh
necklace and the blood
rose blooming
from its face. We ate vegan
corn snax in the shade pool
of a parasol amidst little yellow
flags planted between
the graves to warn the living

about the pesticide spraying. We wore khakis
for hunting
or desert camouflage or urban
warfare if the city
of the about-to-be
dead built itself up
from mud. Wink—we know
what that means. For we have lain
our pale carcasses upon
Hawaii's sandy shores, made by
parrotfish pooping out small
coral bits—I mean it—the female redlip
parrotfish is called "loose bowels"
in Hawaiian. It's hard to hold
in the mind the multitude
of mouths and anuses it takes
to keep this place up. The word *shit*
means "separate," as in to cast off
from the body, and is thus cousin
to "conscience" and "science."
I really liked the guy who came
to deal with the rat issue. Jen said
we were flirting. He spoke
with respect about the smarts of rats,
who are pretty savvy with the traps. He said

someone nearby was poisoning ours,
and showed me how the droppings glow
with an iridescent green hue—that's
how you know the poison's working.
The German word for *poison*
is "gift," same in Danish, Swedish, and Dutch,
from the Greek *dosis* for dose—a giving.
I heard the trap snap at night
just as I was drifting off to sleep.
It made me jump. Rat screams
are ultrasonic—above human hearing.
A group of rats is called a *mischief,*
from the French for "bring to grief."
I put my ear down to dirt just like Darwin
to hear the stamp of little rat feet. The worms'
only developed sense is touch,
Darwin wrote. They are essentially
blind and completely deaf. He found
this out by blowing at them
on a whistle and then on a bassoon.
He determined they have a feeble
sense of smell because his bad
breath did not faze them. Can't you
see old Darwin with that grizzled
face fur puckering vapors onto moist

worm skins in his study? What a weirdo!
The worms though can sense
the faintest of vibrations
through the soil. They know
the world by feel—like living fingers
dispersed throughout earth, but with
intelligence, as Darwin could attest,
by the creative and discerning ways
they tuck leaves into their burrows.
He noted that the lack of sense organs
does not preclude high mental function,
and compared the worms to Laura
Bridgman, a woman from New England,
very famous in her time, both blind
and deaf, who learned to read and write,
and performed these tasks
before an audience. Like rats,
earthworms arrived in North America
with the colonists—few
native worms existed, and the English night
crawlers and red marsh worms invaded, undermining
through slow centuries the northern forests,
eating up the decomposing leaves and tiny
bodies on the surface that the young trees and
the small plants need for sustenance, so that

fewer seedlings can survive. Maybe our "great
outdoors" is geriatric, in decline, like Darwin
when he wrote about the worms, his last
book before he died. His gift was his
obsession for detail and his riches,
which let him spend the hours
plotting worm poop with a ruler.
He observed over thirty-seven years
how a stony field he owned
transformed to soft grass not by
plow or planting but by worms,
casting their waste off
from their bodies, so that English farmers say
things tend to "work their way
down" through the soil, but ancient
Roman villas and orgy sites
and massacres did not sink,
they vanished beneath
the English picturesque—all worm shit.

III.

I tell you this, dear whoever
might be out there, reading with

your eyes or with
your fingers, to make clear—
I know who you are. Bring your
lovely bug bag over here, true
dream clown, my mischief
in make-up. Lie down. We can relieve
our faces in soil—we don't
even need the mall. *I made*
this. I
made this say the
bodies gone under, lit
by the silver threads
of poison pointing like lightning
toward all the earth mouths
wedged open. *I made this.* We
above—we rub ourselves
in conscience, in
science—our gifts, like a Trojan
clown car to deliver
all of us. *I made this.*
Let us
go now fore-
founding fathers, doctors of every
knowledge. Let us go
blind and deaf

in dirt, so we can feel
for the worms
pressing up
with their infinite guts

The things you loved

I lived to haunt you. To ask
you to hold this oldest
piece of human
DNA beneath
your tongue—it's shit
dug up from wave
-cut caves in the Summer
Lake basin of Oregon, mixed
with red fox, wolf, coyote—animals they
ate or later came to pee
on their remains. Hold this and think
the thing you love
the most what you most want
inside you, mixed in
with your excrement in fifteen
thousand years when someone
digs it up. Think
the thing you loved so much
you conjured it in labs to live
inside the flesh of every animal to saturate
your own well-fatted flanks, king
of all the creatures. So these
must be the names for things you loved
so much you peed on all the earth
and all its living things which you then ate

to concentrate its thickest dose inside
your pearl-white fat and rearrange your
DNA and gene expression: aldrin, dieldrin, DDT,
mirex, toxaphene, and TCDD. Heptachlor, hexa
-chlorobenzene, and the PCBs nestled in your
genes with you and chlordecone and the hexa
-chlorocyclohexanes. The mark
of all you loved.

Sorry

for Andrea Murray

The albatross hardly showed up
in that poem. I cleaned out
after it the whole time weeping, mouth
so dried out I had to suck from my own
salty blindness to say I'm sorry
about all the screaming
Jeezy fans in the bank
that used to be your bedroom, I mean
Jesus, screaming Jesus
fans where you shared your last love
with your last lover before she died. That was low,
I know, like Subway low, like bread puffed up
with yoga mat chemicals. Yes I did
steal everyone's detournement I did it
last summer in my sleep on fire
on the land line just a normal
phone call carrying the voice of that
albatross with its stinking breath
from the afterlife. I'm inside it still
falling down to my tiny library
of angel-headed monster cells weeping in
their cancer juice shooting chapbook
after chapbook at Justin
Bieber screaming we love you please
don't get up just for us your fans

forever kickboxing gods in the face so you can relax
with your sizzurp. I drop these names
so my young friends will
not forget me. Here's one: the Jewish refugee who stood
on a street corner in London in 1933. He used to soak in the tub
for three hours a day to get ideas. This day the idea
struck him standing on a street corner in London for a nuclear
chain reaction, which he quickly patented. He wrote his own
Ten Commandments: Number 4. "Do not destroy what you
cannot create." Number 5. Untranslatable German pun. Hmm.
Things that make you go *hmm* to quote . . . you know, quoting
. . . you know. The man, Leo Szilard, slapped
his lizard gloves against his thigh, fist
bumped Einstein and went off
to build that bomb. Ok, no that's historically
irresponsible. Please don't repeat my errors
Justin Bieber don't repeat
your own. Please don't patent your own sizzurp cups out of
Styrofoam. No really, I worry, I'm lying here with this
stinking albatross carcass. It was never a burden
in the poem, it never had that physical heft. The bird
around the neck is more like Hester Prynne, the 1995
Demi Moore version, the scarlet A—a mark
of guilt but not even subtle or symbolic, like, wow, I know
what you did last summer, it's hanging there rotting

on your chest. For real, I know what you did. You can
dress it up with a patent and drown it in
cough syrup. I can still smell it.

I heart

I forgot to put the heart
emoticon in that poem a fat
webbed meat-raw pump—it's so
post-emo early
nineties *Ghost*
the movie where the mother
fed her infant only cow
heart blended into liquid where
the farmer scientist leaves the lamb
on spindly legs to starve upon
the federal research field Nebraska. Who
knew the lamb inside my teeth was really
babies?! I thought that it was just another
moving picture, just another
name for meat. Like when the lion
lies down with the lambs. Wink. When the sea
lion pups washed up by the thousands
on the golden coasts of
California where I'm always writing
thank-you notes to
sound-free sense vibrations *good* so
good good good . . . Who said
that rhythm long precedes
the meaning—*is*
the meaning first the first stirred

sense, the sense that worms make, lambs
when curled up still inside their ewe
skin all the little lambs that twinkle
still like woolly stars still
born as starving sea
pups flood the fields of dark
red farm
states carpeted
with hearts. O coasts
of all
my wants, I want
to wash this slime off
of my hands so I can
text the world
a constant stream
of heart emoticons. I love
you lambs the sea
lions curled like lowing
cow mouths meat
with cream a rain of baby
fat I love you
puppies kitties Easter
chicks that fall like falling
stars of fluff. I hunger
for your touch O fevered

fading movie
of the world, a pulse
I thought
I felt. I make that shape,
thumbs pressed together
pointed downward, fingers
curled in toward each other, not
like a prayer, like
a heart, like
Taylor Swift
I heart. I eat
my heart
out that's
my *yes*—my yes
means *yes* I eat
my little
thumping lamb heart
out—my yes
to the meat
on top.
It eats
out all
the rest

I love you I love you I love
you wound
trace on
skin like, duh,
a scar
the size of
Cincinnatus, leader of the Roman army who only wanted
to go back to farming. I grow my own food, too, Cincinnatus,
but I can't believe I took so long to understand that
I was dead. Like everything alive. So I get out of work early,
cram myself onto your thighs at that best spot for licking
clean the snapshot of the albatross
caught on a fishing line dragged down into the water still
alive its six-foot wings so piteous, ridiculous, the figure
Baudelaire used for the poet—a real aggrandizement. No
human is ever as beautiful or intelligent as an albatross,
its name already a mistake from the Portuguese
Alcatraz for pelican, better known for the prison island,
which is why Bill
Gates insists I capitalize it. You are always here haunting
my poetry, you Boomer
Empire humans who thought you'd die in nuclear war so
went ahead and killed the world. We who came of age
in the neon afterglow 80s just
bought everything you sold. We strung our

prison islands out across the world, and now our wound
-faced offspring won't stop licking
the glossy pictures of that decade. They want
to pretend to be
alive they're so
in love

Nature poem

Ghost is just
the oldest word
for stranger
(anger)—standing
under fruit trees snowing
eyes back
to your eyes like they were flowers
or an anus
on an anthill—that's a metaphor
for life—the whole
heart growing
on its stalk. Enjoy your dirt.
Crow flow. Ant boil. You need
not always be
so fragile. You
can be enmeshed, sprout
your fruit flesh
in a pot. Fundraiser. Hospital
bill. Broken
endless mouth with fucked-up teeth.
Eating turf. Surf. Flag slap on the pole.
Bloodstained dress of yes. Labor
out the flesh of presidents inside
their armored Beasts, alive
means just to be

a better shot
-up fist bump. You?
woke up? You bet
the stain that never fades
gap-toothed and chocked
-up full of fish (my flesh)—the oceanic
white tip once among the most
abundant blood-lit
skins on earth—now any
flesh means only
"entry" and "owned already." Yes
I always only have that one snake word
to speak—bird a flash of reptile bones
pecking around inside me—all those
mobile mouths—the diaper with the Disney
princess on its ass—broken condom—
hypodermic—little seed burst
junk tree—filthy feet—here's a picture
of your future, nature. I was raised
inside a lab to pipe your
organ out in your
last church, by which
I mean *je suis* the swollen
superfunded site
of total want

I was born
because of love
inside a weapons lab.
The End—
Omega
Bridge—connects
the town, the little
boxes lit along
the cliffs. For love
the men awake
and cross
the bridge to labor
on their bombs
for love. For love
becomes a body
in the world. And fear.
A fear comes with it
to the world, a cry
in air burst first
from lungs. And grief,
the instant born,
the shape of what
will come, the shape
of what they'd seen. Become
then students of

the sun, to will that
fire here to burn. The bomb
makers always burned
with so much love—the father
pillars of my child self
in church who prayed
the sun to earth
to burn up
everything
for love. For love
-fused fear.
For grief.

II.

SENTENCES

Today is the day the U.S. dropped an atomic bomb on the people of Hiro-
shima. Russia is poised to invade Ukraine. A forest fire is burning in the
gorge, and I-84 is slow coming into the city. The heat will bring Oregon
winemakers a record harvest. "America Needs Its Farmers," my father
declared the other night at dinner, as if in caps, a retired physicist born
in Iowa. Farmers call themselves producers. Once I heard a farmer from
Iowa call himself an outdoor manufacturer. The news reports this day on
Zach Danger Brown's attempt to make potato salad that raised $55,000
on Kickstarter. He is using the money to throw a concert to alleviate
hunger in Central Ohio. One of my father's titles during his thirty-some
years at Los Alamos was Director of Threat Reduction. I keep a list in
my head of poetry books I want to read. Chris Nealon *Heteronomy,* Fred
Moten *The Feel Trio,* Caroline Bergvall *Drift,* and all of Hopkins just for
summer. A Russian mafia gang stole 1.2 billion username and password
combinations. Ebola represents the desire of a virus to become immortal.
Russia is massing troops on the border, a spacecraft is following a comet
to "touch it and smell it." The Dow is up but due to crash. A *U.S. person*
can refer to a legal "alien" or a corporation. The definition of a *crone* is an
old woman who is thin and ugly. I enjoy central air conditioning, a not-
too-common luxury in Portland. The FBI considers Dearborn, Michi-
gan, a place of interest because of the predominance of immigrants from
Afghanistan and Pakistan. Dearborn is named after Thomas Jefferson's
Secretary of War Henry Dearborn, a general during the American revo-
lution. Women in Hiroshima received flash burns on their skin in the
patterns of their kimonos. The mafia gang consists of a bunch of

20-something boys in south central Russia. No one implies the government was involved but Russian police do nothing. Consumers have most to fear. During World War II, the U.S. firebombed 67 cities in Japan, dropping 40,000 pounds of napalm. A map online shows the cities and their American equivalents in population level: *Cleveland, New York, Chattanooga.* I forgot to add Basho's *Narrow Road to the Deep North,* in which he wrote about walking for five months through remote regions of Japan praised by ancient poets for their beauty, including what is now Fukushima. Pattie McCarthy made me cry at two poetry readings in a row with her poems about being a mother. That the U.S. firebombing of Tokyo killed more people than both bombs dropped on Hiroshima and Nagasaki has become a truism of history. Every breath I drew from birth canal to about age 22 was made possible by nuclear war. *Lexington, Macon, Montgomery.*

In 1899, several nations gathered in the Hague for a peace conference and agreed to prohibit attacks on undefended towns. The comic depicted a bombing alert in Israel going off as the radio in the cab played the Pharrell song "Happy." It's the same song she said played in the cab on the way to the airport for our trip to Hawaii. The word *hibakusha* (被爆者) means explosion-affected people. It has no equivalent in English. A historian named Alex Wellerstein created the map of bombed Japanese cities with their U.S. equivalents: *Butte, Charlotte, Columbus.* He took the data from a set of maps made in the 1940s by the U.S. Army Air Forces, whose leaders felt the atomic bombs got too much credit for ending the war. A normal human respiration rate is called *eupnea* from Greek *eu* for "well" and *pnoia* "breath." It also is called quiet breathing or resting heart. At this point it seems a given that I will not be a biological mother, although technically it is still possible. Yukiyo's mother, a second generation hibakusha, died of cancer last year—bladder cancer I think—Yuki can barely speak of it, and after all I hardly know her. I read on History.com that the U.S. pilots bombing Tokyo got nauseous from the smell of burning flesh, and mists of blood darkened their windscreens. *Corpus Christi, Des Moines, Oklahoma City.*

I'm already thinking of lunch even though it's still morning here in Portland. I need to resist snacking. At the Hague, nations agreed to prohibit the launching of projectiles or explosives from the air with balloons or "other new methods of a similar nature." This agreement came five years before the first airplane flight. The U.S. and Great Britain refused to ratify it. Some hibakusha were not born at the time of the bomb but existed inside the bodies of their mothers. *Omaha, Middleton, Hartford.* In Gaza the family's 90-year-old grandmother asked when she dies to be buried beneath the mulberry in the yard because it's not safe to go to the cemetery.

"Here We Go Round the Mulberry Bush" is an English folk song from the nineteenth century with parallels across northern Europe. It is a children's song but may have been invented by female prisoners. The crone personifies old age; she often has a sinister power. Firebombing involves the use of incendiaries—metal cases filled with thermite or magnesium that burn at temperatures exceeding 1200 degrees. The point is to start uncontrollable fires that burn very hot and fast, spreading further and doing more damage than conventional explosives. *Peoria, Rochester, San Jose.* When a person is excited or upset in movies another person will say "Breathe!" but really what they mean is take deep breaths, breathe more slowly. Yuki sewed replicas of the Fat Man and Little Boy bombs out of kimonos worn by hibakusha and strands of her own hair. In the last month at least 1,800 people in Gaza have died, 72% civilian, according to the United Nations. Israel says it has killed 900 terrorists. Massacre is a word of unknown origin but it might be from the Old French for slaughterhouse. The people of Gaza have no bomb shelters, and a fence controlled by Israel surrounds the border. *Tucson, Tulsa, Waco.*

Human respiration is measured by counting the rise of the chest. It is also important to note whether the person struggles. A typical rate for an adult is 12–20 breaths per minute. Children breathe more—they take more breaths than adults do, especially babies. Yuki exists in the gap between U.S. person and U.S. citizen because she refuses to take the required tests. I take a carrot from the fridge—a golden carrot grown in California—and wash it in tap water from the sink. I'm getting older and my metabolism is slowing, which means in physical terms that my muscles are starting to waste away and the mitochondria in my cells convert food to fuel more slowly. *Greensboro, Augusta, Davenport.* About 1,200 U.S. citizens died in Hiroshima—Japanese-Americans caught in Japan by the war and a few dozen U.S. soldiers who were prisoners. That song "Wiggle" captivates me with its spacey flute riff despite its extreme objectification of female anatomy. Then I tolerate "Graceland" when it comes on because doesn't it have some duende? They say losing love is like a window in your heart. Everybody sees you're blown apart, everybody sees the wind blow. Mitochondria have their own DNA, and some scientists think they may have once been independent beings. Images from Hiroshima have sublimated into popular culture: People walked slowly with arms outstretched, their skin hanging off in strips like movie zombies. A soldier in Hiroshima touched his comrade still standing at attention and he crumbled to ash like a vampire under Buffy's stake. *Chicago, Cambridge, San Diego.*

No one knows exactly how many people died in World War II. Maybe 60 million. The vast majority—three-quarters—were civilian. The official definition of noncombatant in the Geneva Conventions is anyone not taking a direct part in hostilities, including medical personnel and military chaplains, but critiques of bombing often focus on the deaths of women and children. As a type the crone shares characteristics with the hag. *Springfield, Boston, Topeka.* The "Wiggle" video has 179,168,744 views on Youtube. Snoop Dogg appears looking through a giant pair of binoculars with sand grains on the rim. In Hiroshima, the bomb blew off people's clothes, and in some cases their skin, making them feel ashamed. The nurse counted my breaths while she pretended to take my pulse so I wouldn't become self-conscious and change my breathing. She did not tell me my respiration rate so I had to guess. I picked 15. I used this number to calculate how many breaths I took in the first 22 years of my life. *Lincoln, Saint Joseph, Battle Creek.* Of course a significant part of these years I was a child and would have breathed much more, twice as much, and sometimes I ran, played soccer, danced, got nervous, scared, excited, or sick. But I went with 15 to calculate a ballpark number and because I am not very good at math I wrote out each step, or I could say math does not come easily to me as a language or that I lack an intuitive feel for numbers or when it comes to numbers I don't trust my instincts. *Duluth, Evansville, Ft. Wayne.* People of Hiroshima thought their city might have been spared from firebombing because so many Japanese-Americans lived there. Quincy likes to eat the ends of the carrots when I'm done. He's sitting on his bed and trying not to whine.

The first bombs were dropped from the air on All Saints' Day, November 1, 1911, when a pilot in the Italian forces threw grenades at an encampment of Turkish soldiers. The "Wiggle" video features a pool party with dancing women and very fast—almost too fast to catch—frames of ugly white people. An old lady dances through in a floppy black that. Then a bald guy in a purple jacket, acting cartoonishly confused by all the dancing. A corpulent guy rips off his shirt and waves his hands in the air. Later the grandma pops up from under the covers of Jason Derulo's babe-filled bed, smiling lasciviously. Three civilians have died in Israel so far. Israelis use a smartphone app called Red Alert that tells them when to take shelter. *Sacramento, Santa Fe, Savannah.* Survivors of

Hiroshima used cultural referents to try to give some meaning to what they saw. One man wrote "There were objects that appeared to be lumps of flesh lying on the ground. Some of these squirmed from time to time like exhibits in a freak show at a fair ground." Yuki visited Fukushima when she went home to Japan. She created a folding screen made out of kimonos with calligraphy of Basho's poem about his visit there in the 17th century. Nations renewed the Hague peace conventions in 1907 prohibiting bombing from the air, and planned a second conference for 1914, but World War I intervened. *Madison, Little Rock, Kenosha.*

I read on a Yahoo music blog that the flute in the "Wiggle" song is a toy. Jason Derulo's producers Rick Reed and Axident went into a Party City when the group stopped at Starbucks on the way to their recording session. After the bomb, Hiroshima became lush with green plants. The insect predators all had died, but maybe also, some scientists thought, the radiation sparked plant roots to grow. Many people in the West, including the U.S. secretary of state John Kerry, compare Russia's annexation of Crimea with Hitler's invasion of Poland, which sparked World War II. *Fort Worth, Galveston, Pontiac.* I am thinking of treating myself to an Aranciata soda even though it's four Weight Watchers points. I don't usually buy sugar soda, but it was on sale at the store. The pool party in the "Wiggle" video includes an ice sculpture of a headless and legless female torso. Paul Simon got a lot of criticism when *Graceland* came out because he recorded the album in apartheid South Africa. 173,488,000 is the number I came up with of breaths I took from birth to age 22. If the atomic bomb test failed at Trinity, the code message would have been "It's a girl." *Toledo, Baltimore, Miami.*

The New York Times shows only the hand of one of six infants killed in Gaza. It does look dead—waxy and yellow, also smudged with black and blood. I think I should just count all the breaths of my whole life, so we can basically double the original number to 346,896,000. My father used to help me with my math homework; I had to bring a clean yellow legal pad and two sharpened pencils to the table. I wanted to bring Yuki's kimono bombs to Los Alamos to display. *Long Beach, San Antonio, Richmond.* The word *crone* comes from the old French for dead meat. I told J we should really change our banking passwords because of the young Russian men. Blood orange is the best kind of Aranciata soda to get because of the color, which is created with black carrot and paprika, according to the can. The female torso ice sculpture seems also to be a fountain—water pours down a channel where the spine would be. Germany firebombed Warsaw, and then Coventry, London, and other English cities. The UK firebombed many German cities, most notoriously Hamburg and Dresden. When I was young, around 20, I felt a strong urge to have a lot of babies—five or more. My father told me that no president of the U.S. or Russia would ever take the nuclear missiles aimed at one another off of high alert. *Utica, Waterloo, Stockton.* Lots of people supported Paul Simon for featuring black South African artists on *Graceland*, even though musicians were boycotting the country. Yuki is somewhat younger than I am, so she will have fewer breaths. Maybe next time I see her I will secretly count the rise and fall of her chest.

The Soviet Union lost more non-combatants in World War II than any other nation, 10 million, mostly Ukrainians, whom the Nazis planned to exterminate. China is second, with 7.5 million and Poland third, 5.7 million. Cultivated carrots originated in Afghanistan. Black carrots are more common in Asia. Jason Derulo's name is actually spelled Desrouleaux— he is the son of Haitian immigrants. I felt ashamed for bursting into tears in the middle of the restaurant with my father. Civilian means non-military, subject to civil laws, and by extension polite: "having the courteous manner of the citizen as opposed to the soldier." In the "Wiggle" video partygoers lick water dripping off the rear end of the female torso ice sculpture. Shots of this appear several times from different angles— from the side, underneath and especially from the top looking down the crack where the water runs off. It was not just the way he eviscerated my opinions that made me cry; it was that he spoke with a tone of authority that reaches right through my umbilicus about a nightmare world I don't want to live in. *Portland, Los Angeles, Salt Lake City.*

In the 1920s, Britain dropped bombs from the air to "police" rebellious people in Iraq, Afghanistan, and India. The U.S. for years kept silent about South Africa's racist apartheid regime because the country had huge stores of uranium, a byproduct of gold mining. The crone is marginalized by her exclusion from the reproductive cycle, and her proximity to death places her in contact with occult wisdom. *Grand Rapids, Sioux Falls, Knoxville.* The Health Ministry in Gaza has become more efficient over the years about collecting data on people killed in attacks. The online list of cities repeats Wheeling twice. It is a city in West Virginia with a regional population of about 150,000. It is also a town of about 40,000 in suburban Chicago. Military and political leaders maintained the myth of bombing only military targets throughout World War II. The official presidential announcement of the atomic bomb described Hiroshima as an "important Japanese army base." In a piece published in the journal *Aufgabe,* Shonni Enelow wrote: "I became both more cynical and also more aware of the cataclysmic sincerity that characterizes even our most banal delusions." This is a record of sentences from August 6.

Shout at the devil

The young woman who cuts my hair tells me I have a nice-shaped skull—good to know if I get cancer. My mother says she preferred cancer to ending up in Las Vegas. She means the small town in New Mexico—home of the state mental hospital. She says the estrogen pills the doctor gave her in menopause kept her sane. "Cancers are all about home," I read on astrology.com. "They are maternal, domestic, and love to nurture others." The word *home* links to a big box store offering a Black Friday sale on clothes washers.

I press obsessively on a tiny lump in the inner side of my left breast. Women who have not had a child have a higher risk of cancer because their breast cells are "immature," I learn on breastcancer.org. Immature cells are more sensitive to estrogen, as well as hormone-disrupting chemicals. "Your first full-term pregnancy makes the breast cells fully mature and grow in a more regular way." I consider that my breast cells are stuck in an arrested teenage state. I consider that this makes them more vulnerable to chemicals freely used in shampoos, cosmetics, lotion—for example to make the scent of something sweet linger on the skin. The site lists steps women can take to manage themselves and reduce their risk of cancer. It includes the usual: don't get fat; eat vegetables; don't smoke or drink.

When I was in junior high I styled myself a headbanger. Metal seemed to match—more than New Wave—my free-floating anger, my desire for gendered power. Those men wore high heels and makeup, they were my models. I layered on blue eyeliner, teased and sprayed my hair, and wore parachute pants with lots of zippers. Mötley Crüe's "Shout at the Devil" became my twelve-year-old anthem—the sickish guitar riff, the guttural "shout!" of the chorus, and Vince Neil's snarly scream expressed my inner emotional world. I didn't think about who the devil might be, I just wanted to shout and scream against some dark power.

I fended off—mostly—the constant, pestering attention of ninth-grade boys who read my look not as an embodiment of my inner rage but of sluttiness, that I was ready for sex. I wanted to be Vince Neil; the Vince Neils at my school wanted to fuck me. One called me "milky mama" because of my breasts. Another appointed himself my boyfriend and waited by my locker in-between classes to try and suck my face. Once Mrs. Welch, the aged social studies teacher, witnessed this. She cornered me, hissing "I don't ever want to see you doing that again." He was, you know, "trouble," a mixed-race boy with a Jimi Hendrix afro. I had long ago been sifted by the filters of race and class into the category of "good girl." I feared him, for sure, but her weird aggression repelled me. I didn't know, I had no idea, how deeply I bore in my teenage body the fruiting violence of an ancient history.

*

At the coffee shop I pick up a flyer announcing 99Unite is hosting a $50 dinner to commemorate Occupy Wall Street. Someone has crossed out the price and dropped it to $32.50. I've been driving around aimlessly in the fog all morning thinking about purchasing something to kill the ants in my home. I don't want to kill them, really. In *Journey to the Ants,* the scientists Bert Hölldobler and E.O. Wilson say that ants have among the most complex and sophisticated social organization of any living beings. Their colonies consist almost entirely of females; males exist only for mating—then they die or are killed or kicked out by the females. Ants have survived for 100 million years—far longer than humans—and have spread across the planet, establishing themselves on every continent and in just about every ecological niche. They are also all over my house— little black ants, which people here call sugar ants, probably *Tapinoma sessile,* a native species. I brush them off my keyboard as I type. They are moving in a line along the rug and have fanned out in the food cupboard. Last week when she stayed with us, Sue kept plucking the tiny black insects off her body. She held it together pretty well, considering how much I know she can't stand all things that creep and crawl.

I empty the shelves of food. Dark ant specks float in the honey. Colonies consist of thousands of females and the queen, who in this species lays one egg a day. I think they are living inside the walls, erupting forth when the crumbs and drips get dense enough to signal them. I've heard about villages in Africa where the people just clear out when the driver ants sweep through. They let the ants do the spring cleaning—devouring everything in their paths, dead or living.

A new book says people who live in villages are most happy. I guess, if you get to choose your own village people. I prefer anonymity to being burned at the stake for my perversions. During a recent ant outbreak, Juliana happened to be staying at our house. The ants were massing right in my office where she would sleep—no doubt because I am a slob. I mean I can't stop the wheels of production just to keep my body going, so I let food dribble to the floor as I stare into the computer screen, trading my intellectual labor for money. I set an ant bait out by the floorboard and pretty soon the black bodies started to converge on it in a ring—the last ant supper. Later, in *Misanthropocene* Juliana and Joshua Clover wrote: "Fuck everyone who has bought a big bag of ant poison because ants have a social stomach and you are one selfish motherfucker if you can't let them have the very small amounts of food they want to share equally among themselves."

They are right of course. But Jen is sanguine about all of this. She says she doesn't think of it as killing but as pruning the superorganism that is the female ant colony. I like this image—it's got a charm to it, it suggests caring for the ants, sculpting them into something appealing— but I'm not convinced by it. "I think you've got a situation you need to deal with," said Sue, in her most commanding voice, with just a tinge of hysteria. Lindsay says cinnamon repels them, and Laura suggests vinegar. Brian tells me chalk dust works because they don't like to walk through it—it clogs up their chemical sensors. But chalk dust? Is that something academics just pick up? As you can see, I've consulted with a lot of poets about this, lady ants of the future. I know you will outlive this brief human interlude of murder.

*

At the Alice Notley symposium in Oakland, Cathy Wagner gave a paper on houses. She said "Houses are negative space carved out of future time we might have spent otherwise," and I felt like I'd been stabbed in the chest, or maybe eaten borax—my mouth got dry and my stomach hurt. Ants, is that what it feels like? It turns out no one really knows how borax works on the ants. It causes them to starve by disrupting their digestion, but "the mode of action" remains a mystery. Maybe it kills the microbes in their guts, which they need, just like us, to break down food. So the ants eat but they can't get any nutrients out of the sugary ooze. Borax exploits the ants' social stomach—they bring it back to the nest to regurgitate for their sisters, and everybody dies. But sometimes an ant dies before she can get back, and then I watch another ant taste and smell all around the body with her antennae, seemingly tenderly, and then gather it up to carry off. Ants can't tell another ant is dead until she starts to smell, and they leave their dead outside the nest. Maybe this one just wants to collect this stilled piece of herself—like if your finger got cut off you'd want it back. I know, I'm anthropomorphizing. I filter the world through my own white, female, queer, worker drone, non-reproductive being.

A permaculture guru I heard speak once likened a house to slow release fertilizer as it imperceptibly crumbles back into dirt. This is calculated to be a horrifying thought if one considers all the toxins encased within a domicile—the lead paint, the asbestos tiles, the polyurethane soaked hardwoods, toilet and tooth bleachers, insect killers. Now think about all those toxic boxes sprawled across all that soil. But humans are slow release fertilizers too—how one soaks up poisons and leaks them back to the world. I mean the "cruel optimism" Cathy talked about at the Notley conference, citing Lauren Berlant's concept of the quest for the good life: property, money, credit, consumables. How one is already dead—breathing, but foreordained to suck up the deadly sugar juice of capital. It's the only food left, or rather, there's all this "food" lying around in gleaming pools so easy to dip into. One might sometimes think "I really shouldn't eat this," or have this nagging feeling that something might be wrong, but most often forget to think at all and just keep falling, open-mouthed, through that glistening surface of goo.

*

At the coffee shop I buy a locally brewed kombucha called Love to get me through this foggy work morning. Every day when I wake up I do a healing reiki meditation that CAConrad taught me, and I hold in my mind the images of all the women I know who have cancer—they range in age from one year old to eighty. I think of the women cancer has killed, leaving raw pain trails through the lives of people I love: Alicia's best friend, Paul's mother, Ethan's mother, Carol's mother, Jill's mother, Deborah's sister, Kathy, Stacy, Julie, my aunt Diana, Leslie, Lesley. The list gets longer. I hold them in my mind and feel the warm buzz between my palms. Then I apply the warmth to my own body, over my left breast.

*

This morning, all the way up the hill to the dog park, I watched a mob of crows attack a red tail—the dark bodies of the crows silhouetted against the blue, the pale belly of the hawk flashing in sunlight as it dove and veered. I guess the crows have survived so well by being such assholes. I know E.O. Wilson's theories of sociobiology are controversial, but I find his notion of *homo sapiens* as an invasive species clarifying. He points out that humans evolved in Africa and Asia, and these are the only places where people have not yet driven the large animals into extinction. Elephants, rhinos, tigers, lions, and humans all evolved together, and all developed defenses to one another. As *homo sapiens* spread out across the planet, they encountered animals that had no defenses, and they ate them. The first to go, says Wilson, are "the big, the slow, and the tasty." Giant lemurs in Madagascar, moas in New Zealand, Mediterranean tortoises, the woolly mammoth in Europe, the massive Irish elk—all that mobile meat.

*

In a few days I'll travel to Hawai'i to read ecopoetry. This requires jet engines blasting out flaming gases across 2,592 miles of open ocean to the planet's most isolated clot of humanity. In the Hawaiian airlines magazine, *Hana Hou!,* which means "do it again," I will read about the islands' ant invasion. Hawai'i has no native ants, but 58 species now inhabit the archipelago, including four of the top five invasive species: the yellow crazy ant, the Argentine ant, the big-headed ant, and the little fire ant. The ant of most concern, I will learn, is the little fire ant (LFA). The state has formed an agency—the Ant Lab—to eradicate this tiny insect, so small it is barely visible. The article quotes Ant Lab head Cas Vanderwoude, an Australian entomologist: "My absolute passion is my extreme hatred for this particular ant . . . It's personal."

The little fire ant landed in Hawai'i in 1999 with a shipment of palms from Florida. Scientists could figure this out because the queens are all clones of the original, and all the male ants are clones of the father, so they could just match the ant genes. LFAs form colonies around queens, but instead of warring with one another like most ants, LFA colonies cooperate, forming supercolonies. The LFAs in Hawai'i are clones of the ones in Florida—they form a single four-thousand-mile supercolony.

Some research suggests that LFAs clone themselves in order to survive in what Hölldobler and Wilson call "the shifting wreckage created by people." In its native forests of Central and South America, the ant— *Wasmannia auropunctata*—reproduces sexually and does not dominate.

But when people spread them to new places, LFAs start creating clones and take over. In some areas of the tropics, Hölldobler and Wilson write, they form "a living blanket of ants."

One key weapon in the war against LFAs in Hawai'i involves training homeowners to "Bait and Blast"—first lure the lady workers by coating trees, plants, and soil with sticky bait, then follow up a few weeks later with insecticide for good measure. Repeat indefinitely.

*

Being female and being alive are the two greatest risks for breast cancer, according to the Dr. Susan Love Research Foundation. That is because no one understands what complex of damage and chance causes certain cells to clone themselves and take over. The familiar narrative involves genetics, lifestyle, and reproductive status. Often left blank is the fact that hundreds of industrial chemicals spur tumors to grow, or they scramble hormone signals, which can trigger cancer. Some chemicals, like phthalates, pour out of factories by the billions of pounds every year. They are mostly invisible to people—one can't see, smell, or taste them—but they are everywhere.

Phthalates are clear, syrupy liquids, cheaply produced by breaking apart the molecules in fossilized life forms—gas and oil—and forcing them into new shapes. They transform brittle plastic into soft, squeezable objects for every use and desire—rubber ducky, blood bag, dildo. Phthalates go in food wraps, floor tiles, clothing, hair spray, shoes, roofing, car interiors, catheters, wall paints, electrical cords, pesticides, notebooks, and fake leather. In cosmetics, perfume, and lotion, phthalates make the product last and its scent linger on the skin.

People get phthalates in their bodies by breathing air, eating food, and touching things. A U.S. government study of 2,636 people over age six found phthalates in the urine of every one. Women had higher levels of the types of phthalates used in body washes, shampoos, and cosmetics. Other studies link phthalates to what are called "reproductive abnormalities" in newborn boys, like a shorter distance between the anus and genitals—a sign of "feminization" associated with a lower sperm count later in life. The chemicals enter the fetus through the blood of the mother.

Phthalates are hard to test for because they contaminate everything in the laboratory—a phenomenon researchers call the "phthalate blank" problem. One scientist, Alain Lenoir, thought he was encountering the phthalate blank in his studies of ants. He wanted to figure out how ants recognize each other by using their antennae to detect certain scents on other ant bodies. Every ant he studied had phthalates clinging to it. He thought maybe it was just his equipment, so he decided to try testing ants from across the world and to keep them away from lab plastics. Ants from Burkina Faso, Egypt, Greece, Hungary, Morocco, and Spain all had phthalates—not only on their outer parts but spread throughout their bodies.

*

"To write of death is to write of everyone," says Anne Boyer, in her essay "The Sororal Death." She counters a claim by Susan Sontag that, unlike men, women don't die for each other—there is no female equivalent to fraternal sacrifice. "The sororal death," writes Boyer, "is not women dying for each other, but women dying of being women." Boyer calls the sentence "I was diagnosed with breast cancer in 2014 at the age of 41," an ideological one.

*

People started using radiation to destroy cancer cells pretty much as soon as William Röntgen figured out how to create x-rays in 1896. The radiation passed through skin and illuminated bones, but it also caused blisters and burns. A medical student in Chicago named Emil Grubbe decided to try using the rays to burn out the breast cancer inside a woman named Rose Lee. It seemed to work—her tumors withered. Although the cancer bloomed again later and eventually killed her, the practice of blasting tumors with radiation spread.

In the 1930s, a Berkeley physicist named Ernest Lawrence conjured radioactive substances that had never before existed on earth. He made an unlikely twentieth-century alchemist. A blonde, blue-eyed descendant of Norwegian immigrants from North Dakota, he wore round, wire-rimmed glasses, sharply pressed suits, and slicked-back hair with a severe part. A "regular fellow" in the words of his 1968 biographer Herbert Childs, he was "as extroverted and happy as the normal American male is supposed to be." The implicit comparison is with Lawrence's close friend and colleague Robert Oppenheimer—dark, brooding, thin to the point of ghostliness.

Lawrence lusted after knowledge. He wanted to probe all the secrets of atoms, the latest frontier in science. He invented a machine he called the cyclotron, which spun tiny particles around a circular track held in a magnetic field—fast enough to smash into atoms and break them apart. Lawrence only cared about the exotic substances that resulted because of what they could tell him about atoms, but he understood that new sources of radiation might also be useful for medicine, a practical pursuit that brought money from funders.

In 1937, doctors diagnosed Lawrence's mother, Gunda, with cancer in her uterus and gave her three months to live. Lawrence and his brother, a physician, brought her to California to dose her with powerful x-rays from a machine created in Lawrence's lab. The cancer doctor noted that Gunda suffered more from radiation than any patient he had ever known, but that she also was "one of the least complaining." The radiation probably penetrated her pelvis, abdomen, and intestines and burned off the mucus lining her gut—which would make her body unable to process nutrients. She remained sick for a long time, but the x-rays destroyed her tumors. She lived for twenty more years.

The problem, of course, is that radiation kills as well as heals. Grubbe, who pioneered radiation therapy, had his fingers cut off one by one and parts of his face, and he died with tumors filling his body. Lawrence admitted being "deathly afraid of cancer," even before his mother's illness. He took care to avoid the radiation in his laboratories. He refused to have even a chest x-ray.

In 1938, shortly after *Kristallnacht* shattered Jewish communities across Germany, two scientists in Berlin split uranium atoms by bombarding them with neutrons—an event the Jewish physicist Lise Meitner and her nephew Otto Frisch, both living in exile, interpreted to be fission. Once news reached the U.S., Lawrence said he could feel the possibility of an atomic bomb "in his bones," and turned his boundless ambition—and his machines—toward building one. His lab created the first known plutonium, and his methods—enlarged to industrial scale—helped enrich the uranium used in the Little Boy bomb dropped on Hiroshima.

*

In 1971, the year I was born, Richard Nixon declared war on cancer—in part to distract attention from the other war, in Vietnam. Since that time, the cancer industry has boomed. The top ten cancer drugs each made $1 billion in sales in 2010, and cancer research in the U.S. consumes about $15 billion a year. But the causes of cancer remain largely mysterious, and treatment has evolved only modestly. The mainstays remain dousing the body with chemicals and radiation—so that healing the body requires bringing it closer to death. It's an approach that my sister's childhood best friend, whose mother, grandmother, and aunt died from breast cancer and who is now a cancer researcher, once described as "killing an ant with a sledgehammer."

*

When Hawaii's Ant Lab head Cas Vanderwoude said "It's personal," he was perhaps unconsciously alluding to the movie *Jaws 4*, whose tagline was "This time, it's personal." The plot of this movie—universally reviled by critics and audiences—involves a great white shark following the Brody family from New England to the Bahamas to exact revenge on them for their shark-murdering ways. With the family patriarch dead, the film focuses on the mother, Ellen Brody. Ellen develops a psychic connection with the shark that stalks her family—she can sense when the animal is close and getting ready to attack. She decides to sacrifice herself to the shark, but is rescued just in time by her new love-interest Hoagie Newcombe, played by Michael Caine. To finish shooting *Jaws,* the actor famously had to miss accepting his Oscar for *Hannah and Her Sisters*. Caine later said that he didn't mind his part in the *Jaws* flop because it paid for his brand new house.

Sharks hold the throne in pop culture as the ultimate symbols of a merciless, terrifying nature, but as Vanderwoude could attest, it is really ants who are among the über assholes of the earth. They rival humans for dominance—the weight of ants on the planet equals the weight of people, but that weight is distributed across many tiny bodies, making ants far more ubiquitous. Hölldobler and Wilson describe ants as "elegant and pitiless." After a combined eighty years of study, the two scientists concluded that ants are among the most rapacious and warlike of all animals: "The foreign policy aim of ants can be summed up as follows: restless aggression, territorial conquest, and genocidal annihilation of neighboring colonies whenever possible. If ants had nuclear weapons, they would probably end the world in a week."

Ant colonies form such tightly functioning units that people studying them decided that they serve as a single being—not an organism but a superorganism. An organism is a group of cells working in concert to make up a living being. In a superorganism, the individual ants function as cells, and the colony displays a totality of traits and abilities contained within no single individual. "One ant alone is a disappointment," write Hölldobler and Wilson. "It is really no ant at all."

*

What happens in cancer is this: A cell—one of the body's own cells—begins to redirect certain basic cell activities. First is cell division. It starts to clone, copying itself over and over. It induces blood vessels to grow, hijacking the blood supply, and activates the ability to travel around the body. Cancer cells cooperate and evolve as they divide, evading the immune system and resisting drugs. Regular cells have a lifespan—they die after a certain number of divisions—but cancer cells don't. If they didn't kill off their host, cancer cells could keep going, they live forever.

The most prolific cancer cells have been replicating in laboratories around the world since 1951. They belonged to Henrietta Lacks, the descendent of white male plantation owners in Virginia and black female slaves. The mother of five children, including a newborn, Lacks was treated for cervical cancer in the "colored" ward of Johns Hopkins. Doctors used the standard treatment: They sewed glass tubes of radioactive radium to her cervix and packed her vagina with rolls of gauze to hold them in place. But it didn't work. The tumors spread and filled her body, growing over her organs and blocking her bladder. Her suffering was so extreme that nurses tied her to the bed so she wouldn't thrash herself off. She died at age 31. When the autopsy assistant looked into her body she saw so many tumors it was like someone had filled her with pearls.

Scientists took Lacks's cancer pearls and cultured more of them—the first set of human cells to survive outside the body. Cells that grow forever make ideal research tools because scientists can endlessly divide and alter them. People used Lacks's cells to develop the big medical technologies of the twentieth century, including the polio vaccine and chemotherapy. They used them to test the effects of radiation from the atomic bomb. Her cells have a name—HeLa—and they remain central to biomedical research everywhere. They are robust, even for cancer cells— so virulent that scientists refer to them as "weeds" because they invade other collections of cells in the lab.

Scientists have created many tons of HeLa cells, more than ever existed in Lacks's own body. Her family has no claim to them, nor to any of the billions in profits they have generated. The legal precedents are clear on this: Once cells or tissues leave you, you lose all ownership rights to those parts of yourself.

*

Studying a superorganism offers advantages, because a scientist can endlessly divide and alter the colony without killing the whole being. Wilson uses horticultural metaphors to describe this activity, noting that he "trimmed" the colonies of lady leafcutter ants in his laboratory from 10,000 to 200 workers. He writes:

> The advantage of tearing apart the colony and then reas-
> sembling it repeatedly is the same as, say, vivisecting a
> human hand and restoring it repeatedly without pain or

inconvenience to discover the ideal anatomical configu-
ration ... One day we cut off the thumb (painlessly),
ask the subject to perform manual tasks such as writing
or opening bottles, and at the end of the day stick the
thumb back on . . . The next day the terminal digits are
trimmed off . . . and so on . . ."

Hölldobler and Wilson conclude that ants are so successful because of
the power they get from cooperating. Keeping thousands of units func-
tioning as one requires a sophisticated communications network—which
ants achieve by releasing chemicals from their bodies. Each colony has
its own scent and taste. Lady workers bathe themselves in this identity
by constantly licking and smelling their queen and one another.

Supercolonies of ants take this coordination to a whole new level. Argen-
tine ant colonies cover much of California from the Mexican border to
San Francisco. They are part of a global supercolony spread by humans,
with segments in Europe, Japan, and New Zealand. Argentine ants living
centimeters apart in separate supercolonies are constantly at war—the
boundaries between them fill up with dead ant bodies. But drop an ant
from New Zealand into her own genetic colony in San Diego, and she
will melt into the body of her sisters.

*

In junior high, the same year as "milky mama" and the pseudo-boy-friend, the most popular group of girls, the girls who held sway over the whole school, decided they hated me. What happened was this: I shared a bus seat on a school field trip with the boyfriend of the head girl. He said he wanted to make out with me, and he stuck his wet tongue in my ear. Somehow she found out about this, and she massed ranks against me. Every day at school, one by one, girls who used to be my friends would turn their backs and refuse to speak to me. Only a few of my oldest friends from childhood stayed loyal, and I could see them almost physically have to overcome their repulsion—as if I had suddenly become coated in something disgusting.

One day word went around that the head girl was going to fight me after school. She met me on the sidewalk right outside the front doors, and a crowd of kids circled us. We just stared at each other, both frozen, not speaking, for what seemed like several slow, agonizing hours. A bunch of boys, including the ear licker, kept urging us on, almost pleading, "Just hit her, *come on!*" What the boys didn't get was this—there was no need to physically fight. I was already socially dead.

A few years later, in high school, I learned about the internment of Japanese-Americans during World War II. This information stunned me. It was the first time in my sheltered life that I understood my government was capable of evil. I felt a subtle shift in the ground of my being—I could not believe I had survived so long on the planet innocent of these facts. The knowledge that the U.S. government dropped atomic bombs on Hiroshima and Nagasaki, and that my town existed in order to build those bombs, did not arrive in my consciousness in such a jarring fashion—I don't remember "learning" this at all. It's like being raised in a religion, as I was, you don't suddenly learn that there's a god, it's just an awareness you have always had. I remember the gospel, though: The atomic bombs saved lives by shortening the war. The atomic bombs saved lives. This was the glass we looked through from our fortified mesa top, the clear mountain air we breathed, the water that washed through our cells.

*

I'm standing in Portland's yuppie natural grocery. I started out in the gleaming aisles of the superstore, but it sold only a row of evil-sounding ant poisons. I'm looking for Terro, the borax baits, which are called "green" because they are toxic only to insects, not mammals. I can't find any, so I turn to ask a young woman stocking shelves nearby. I feel ashamed to be shopping for ant poison, so I say something stupid: "Do you have any ant murdering juice?" She does not react as if my question is ridiculous, but she needs to consult a coworker—a big guy with a beard. The three of us hunt up and down the aisles—no Terro. All he can produce in terms of an arsenal is a pitifully small-looking wooden mouse trap. So I wander back out in the fog through the parking lot to my car.

Parked next to me is a dented pickup truck, its dashboard covered in notes—white squares of paper scrawled with black ink are taped to every inch. One says something about homework, but it's hard to decipher. Another one says, in clear, big letters "Buy TERRO—ants again." I put my face to the window to get a better look. But the owner has just returned, a middle-aged woman wearing a white fleece vest. She is standing by the driver's side window, staring at me through the cab of her truck. I take a step back with a laugh and start to say something, but she just keeps staring. So I turn quickly and climb behind my own steering wheel.

I drive back to the house that is called mine but is really a structure erected on farmland some sixty-five years ago by an enterprising developer, part of a community called "Charlotte Heights," a name no one uses anymore, if they ever did. It was built out of old growth Douglas fir cut from the mountains nearby. It is covered in asbestos shingles, impervious to fire and decay, but if they break down they release microscopic fibers that lodge in the lungs and spur cancer to grow. Some people lived here for a few years and then left, and then some other people, one family, lived here for five decades, a father and five children but with an ebbing and flowing of women—Mickie, the mother who died of cancer, or maybe that was the later companion Opal who worked with Howard on the railroad, and the last one was Faith, who died in this house. This little bit I have gleaned from the neighbors.

The building is mostly owned now by a massive global financial institution to which I pay interest every month, and a little bit of my debt, in exchange for the fulfillment of the body's need for shelter—a need that has been monetized and transformed into a class of profit-generating commodities and a means of enforcing boundaries—separateness, what keeps things out. The word *shelter* comes from *shield*, a flat piece of wood or metal to protect the body in war, and from a much older root meaning "cut," to break apart.

The truth is that shelter always eventually fails—the tiles crack, a fire starts, the ants thread their nests through the walls.

*

At the discussion that closed the Alice Notley symposium, someone asked Notley about shelter. One of her most celebrated books of poetry is *Mysteries of Small Houses,* in which she investigates chronologically all the shelters of her life. Notley said that she wrote about her houses because they had always been so fragile. The trick, she said, is to see how fragile you can get away with.

I reported this later to Cathy. Her reply was "re: how fragile can you get while still having a shelter—it seems a good rule for souls as well as houses."

I have been thinking about this ever since. I'm not sure what it means—to live in the most fragile house, with the most fragile soul. In the poem "The Howling Saint T-Shirt," Notley refers to her children as "Flow of atoms . . . never my own body." She writes "I need their words for my poems, to speak for a / house we make together that's fragile and strong / shaky." That extension across the line keeps sounding in my mind: fragile and strongshaky—like one word fused together, like a voice might sound, speaking . . . "the kind / Of shaking that keeps you steady"

And then I know. The house must be fragile. That's what makes it infinite—opened to the gaps and the cracks and all that flows through them. And the soul? The word *fragile* came to English late, from the Latin *frangere*, to break. It meant "liable to sin, morally weak." Sin comes from the ancient root for "to be." Take the Devil, old accuser, inside for divine principle. Be undeceived, a mixed thing. Be clear, like a web, almost all hole. Be a way that is not at war.

III.

YOU WERE BORN

The shining part
of shields and weapons and up-
armored trucks. The glitter
sprays of sun I hold
my hands up in, a kind of
scream from dreams I throw
my flame-burnt bird
beak heart. *No hope*
is what the mother told
the press, a tune
that has no words and never
stops. The bullet works
by hitting with such force, the force
of a Mack truck though it's just
a one-inch slug of densest lead,
it leaves a trail like a freeway
crash through bone and flesh
because it flies so fast, it's a
primitive technology, a pointed
bit of soft and silver poison metal
wrapped inside a gleaming
coat of copper. A white man
in a grey suit aiming a gun
in each hand precedes
the news report. It's an ad

for a TV show on TNT
called *Legends*. At the office the old
assistant put a sign up that said Force
Yourself. Force Yourself down
to the ground and spread
your legs and keep
your hands above your head, the cop
kept screaming. A helmet and a gas
mask make the man seem only
weapon. The word *force* means body
of armed men. My town holds
some of the planet's most
dangerous substances that kill
by moving invisibly through cells
and scrambling the atoms that make
up flesh and bone. A mercenary army
guards the stuff with guns. We used to park
at a gate to the lab to make out
and wait, before too long a guard
would come with gun and light and
shine it on our skin
and sometimes let us stay there
steaming up the panes at the edge
of the cliff where the radiation leaked
into rock of hardened ash from an ancient

volcano. They never scared me
once, I never had to think of force from
sunglassed men in uniform, a white
and privileged chick I always cried
if I got stopped and usually I knew
the cop—Officer Grecian, Captain Tom—
church members and friends, they almost
always let me off. The violence I knew
came in much more intimate forms,
without a gun, in homes and cars.
The physicist Otto Frisch wrote
that asking them to stop the work
on the atomic bomb once it began and then
refrain from using it on people would be
like asking a boxer to sense in the heat
of the fight the moment his opponent lost
his strength and started the slide to defeat
and stop pummeling him with his fists
into unconsciousness. Can you hear
the global engine gunning, getting
louder? Once it's out and hot and
loaded up, it's just too hard to stop.

Shhhhhh. This poem breaks down
electron bonds inside you. I'm sorry
for breathing
as we all do
asbestos slivers
from the floor tiles
in the jiu-jitsu dojo. I'm sorry for the human
handpunch to your
poemface. But don't you think
this violent art best proves
our love
for Sister Sledge? I've got all my sisters here
on stakes about
to air kiss you
with flame. My own white hot
karategi absorbs
the war drones of the wealthy
crammed up at this art bar. Sorry
I did burn to ash
all your click baits of the Sirens
riding bikes
across a shark's back. The Internet quiz says I'm an oceanic
white tip, your worst Shark
Week nightmare, known for frenzy feeding
on shipwrecked humans. When I sleep I dream

like sharks
who never sleep. It's stupid
to understand how everything has died and then
try—what—to warn you? Old English
sing has no related forms in other tongues. I've lost
my thread again. We get them back
by snagging them on hooks, slicing off their fins for soup,
and tossing the bleeding body back into the water. Sorry
Earth for having killed you sorry everyone the universe so
sorry, full of sores, the sisters who will never
be my own, the plastic shard
called god. It seems I'm not
the only person on the Internet
to ask if the Titanic people died from sharks. No, they froze
to death of course. I blow
my raft first-class and float, snagging clams and shoving
ice cream down my throat so I can state,
you know, for the record, I never did feel glad
to be here, or if I did I did
in spite of
all of you breeders. JK! I know! Not nice! I'm just jealous
we never could get our own
zygote on the hook
inside me. Oops, confessional territory. Sorry. It's a first
-world problem. I mean everything. It's all

your fault. And mine. But we can still have all the ice cream
we can eat for life. We keep it cool by sending
super-warming gases to the atmosphere. I'm sorry, but you
know those sharks don't care. Let's raise
our instruments and make the best
sounds we can make until we sink. It's a nice thought right,
like a rubber ducky in a snow
-white gi, or is that an angel's robe and golden halo, wisp
of cloud across the final glacier? I know, we can
cram ourselves inside each other's
shark skins, suck on our inhalers and finally spill it all—
just like those four drum beats quick before the first
electric keyboard notes I press to my white ear one
thousand times an hour building through guitar the bass
more strings and horns til those true
sisters break out into song. We *are* family, a family
of sharks who when they get excited even
eat each other, who even try to keep on feeding once
they're disemboweled. OK
here's my confession: I never knew kung fu
I just liked the sounds of words
in my own mouth and struck a pose to feel them out.
You try it too, like getting French-kissed from the inside
by an angel in the light of all the films

we ever cried to. Come on, tell me
everything. Get up everybody. Sing.

Look

O be
hilarious, oh spill
yourself into the general dis
-course, Smurf
mushroom house I hated
before I even opened the Christmas box—all
those creepy blue men in my bedroom. But I pretended
to love them suckled as I was on the code of being female—
don't hurt their famous feelings above all—be dead
before ugly, improper—it means
false, what doesn't fit: My whole skin every cell and synapse
every breath and bit of nourishment leaked to me from
womb onward came courtesy of your shining
tax dollars and our movie
star president's love for Star
Wars—the missile
not the movie. *Lost*
Almost he called it, my father, a joke: Los
Alamos, the cottonwoods, a tree that means
water in the desert you can live there. Lost
Almost it was
his joke it always came
out of his mouth first, we learned everything

out of that mouth—my mother, I had her
body at twelve held
his hand and pretended I owned him
as husband, could I look
old enough for that—could I hold that kind of
superpower? Rage. I didn't understand then
how it could blank one—a woman
much later asking if I worried about getting sick being from
there I couldn't answer I'd never thought of it I didn't know
any sick people who could be me I hated
that woman for her question my dis
-ease, I hated or really feared, we feared the Cave Woman.
She lived in the canyon between the town and the lab
beneath Omega Bridge in a cave everyone
said I never saw her but my friend's mom warned us
be careful my boyfriend drove his V W down at night to try
and find her no one I knew ever did, but U S A
Today reported in 2004 a man living in a cave in Los
Alamos with solar and a grow-op and a glass front door.
They charged him with possession. There is not
a real law I guess against squatting in a government-owned
cave in the richest county in the country. He pleaded
not guilty. The Deputy Fire Chief said he was impressed
with the man's ability to live in such style unseen in the
zone of exclusive Smurfdom sorcerers—the future

is really now remember how you exploded how the boy
said nice books I
mean nice but they need tanning, the reporter said she
appreciated the animal for
how it died without whining. According to *The New York*
[war] *Times* the people of
the richest county Lost Al
-most live eleven years longer, on average, than the people
of the poorest: Clay County, Kentucky. *Hilarious* comes from
Greek for "joyous," *Kentucky* is Iroquois
or Shawnee perhaps for "meadow" or "a shining river in the
midst of it." Let us hang
next to Thomas Jefferson this portrait of the Sampson
Pearlymussel gone extinct in Kentucky in 1984, and the
Disappeared Island Elugelab, vaporized in Earth's first
thermonuclear fire—all part of our national ab
-cessence inside the White
Skull House of cavities for feelings. "I felt," she wrote in her
portrait book of extinct species, "like I
could be the one
to give them a voice." She counted
my breaths as I spoke
from the French: *the no*
turns out to be nothing
but a yes . . . the injunction to look

at what looks back—the one
the gun's still
pointed at

Drone poem

for CAConrad

I have this good sick
sea body to share
come here   plant
your fork between
our wars more
and more last
meals to eat one
another til gleaming
creatures gang
up to watch
our flare in the dark
device set to sniff
for the hot blood
flooding our target
-shaped skins lit
by lasers
from the stars
falling down
where we fuck
in the fuck
-loving grave

Moo

Hello my friends I love you I'm late. Had you
known me when Julius Caesar
knew me you'd say I had evil horns and couldn't stand
the sight of men. I never was any kind
of cool, I ran
hot and awkward and every time I sang
I cried. Now velvety and with only nubs
for weapons I lie softly chewing the food
that will kill me, fattening into the form
of our hero's next meal whereby I
fuel with my body the muscle that shoots
the steal peg in our head. By I I mean obviously
seared meat chunks still mooing in that
epic poem where the women all sit quietly
weaving and bathing
the bodies of men though some do dissemble
and flirt without shame. But the whoring
female servants swing so satisfyingly
from their necks at the end. The goddesses
seem exempt from that crap. But they are
also jocks. Athena leads the slaughter, she sanctifies
Ulysses so we can feel how hot
he is how violent and arrogant and cool
and hot like sexy
hot not blushing

as I always am in this dress
of meat. Meat skirt. I,
my friends
cannot help you, born
into this war to end
all wars that
won and will
go on. I mean our
favorite national tale involves two men
on a dusty street shooting each other with guns. Not
too much plot, so it's easy
to remember, no poets required, just lots
of glistening cuts. Moo, I pose for you
in my shining dress. I'm the flesh
that after it's flayed keeps
crying and crawling back

Poem called More

for Brandon Brown and Evan Kennedy

Every life has its Taylor
Swift relic
bones, I mean the glacier
named for her—it's
melting so we pray
for it. Right? But we flame
too hard for this
neverending war. Stars,
as in, we are
objects of desire, we are
who we R, that is
fucked by the very
air moist with the blood
of the Super Holy™ soldier
telling you this tale: Saint
Francis the archetypal drunken whoring
warrior in shining golden armor stood
bolt upright in his tomb two hundred years
after he died and his blind eyes flashed fire. The Saint
I am is trying to tuck this
into your tiny hip pocket. It's innocent
I promise, a present, all the shells and feathers
of this war with it's stinking
sink hole. But don't worry, for
real, we can bleach all this out

and start over with some new
unpronounceable people and their sparkling
pre-dead soldier teens, you know
like the commercial, "Don't worry
we'll make more." Don't worry. All of this
is ours from shore to shining
neverever. Ever. Like that song Ms. Swift sang for us, the one
that made everybody melt and hold
their hats to their sweaty
hope chests. I built this™, and my drone
reads my mind, like the ships of the ancient Phaeacians. We *are*
getting back together, we can
start over, we will always have
more, which to the Saxons meant *greater,*
stronger, the rights of the Conqueror. We came.
We vino'ed. We karaoked. And you know how
that makes us feel. Like Saint Francis
before he was poor. We believe, clap
your hands. We can always have more.

What the businessman said

the business
-man I shook
hands with
drinking local
whiskey at the
party Christmas
winter I mean non
religious for the
green
group where
his wife
donates her
hours bought
just bought
an old Victorian cheaper
than a Craftsman in
one of Portland's
oldest best said
cost the cost
of doing
business one
cost of
doing
business all of
life of costs

a cost the business
-man made
exercise machines
in China for
the bodies of
Americans
to sweat upon
the muscles heart
and blood vessels
the lungs he said
they never
even counted
labor
costs the labor
lives so cheap it was
the metal minerals
the plastic
parts they had
to calculate the labor
lives so
cheap they didn't
even count

Dear corporate

for Lisa Jarnot

Dear corporate
body I write you
from the rose room
bleeding big chunks
of cash out of
earth *money*
rocks, right? Birth
forth this red sweatshirt
with its blood hood
chewing brain food
to perform up
to snuff the
swallowing eyeball
of capital I mean
Google Street View
I can almost see
myself working
in screenlight
forever dragging that
dirty car part I mean
my body leaking
luck every dawn
shove my eyes
back in place
jam my palm over

chest blank to face
up with prayer face
our bomb's birth
light in air
fucking proof
goddamn
we're still here

You were born

after Joshua Clover and Juliana Spahr's "Misanthropocene"

Oh dear, you were born
with that poison song singing
through your veins and you trail
a wide train
of war where you go: dial up
the chandelier, new
hurricanes swirl, step through the parting
doors into the drugstore, more big
-eyed children amassing at the border. I know
it's not your fault as in
you killed them, you just
killed everything breathing, by you I mean
the sun lamps
we call our lives,
my friends, elegiac,
on auto correct, as they will
have been, having come
so late, after everything can't stop
weeping at the gleaming Apple
flagship. It's a new mode of poetry
called West Melancholy. Google it,
click that link for a pair of lady feet
prancing around in strappy
red Nine
West "Melancholy" sandals to that

Robin Thicke good
-girl beat. You know you
kind of want to buy them now,
they zip up the back, so hot
they're sold out, they're Greek
-ish, called "open-toed
caged booties." What *is*
melancholy but the global
brand rapture, the shining
spew of song from the poison
entrails of all my heroes, who are
you guys—my friends, alive
and in love
with nothing
but partying
at this funeral
for the eighties
glam bands and their simplistic
misogyny, yes, every rose
has its thorn just like every cowboy
sings his sad, sad song
of the good old days
of gunfire
in utero. Once born
in war you have

to live there. But we, me and my
spirit-slut shoes, just pretend
we can keep on bleeding
these horseshoe crabs
of their primordial blue blood.
You read about that on I Fucking
Love Science, right? They're not crabs
at all, but ancient pre-dinosaur sea
spiders, and their blood can detect
even the tiniest trace of evil
microbe invaders on that plastic
apparatus about to be inserted
in your body: pacemaker,
false boobs, hernia net,
hypodermic.
              They come to breed
in shallow seas each spring
in the bay of Delaware, named for the Lord
De la Warr. So the crabs crowd up
in the bay to breed beneath the new
and full moons in the months of May and June,
and the watermen—
the watermen wade in, grab them by the shell
and toss them on trucks
to a lab where lab

people strap them to a steel table, insert a needle
to the heart, drain 30% of the blood,
and send them back to the water of the war. One quart
goes for $15k. It seems fake
but it's
real like the teenage
girl I once saw at the national
zoo pointing
at every sad skin sack in its
bootie cage, pronouncing
"that's fake," a word of London gang
slang from when *to fake*
a man out and out meant
to hurt him
all the way up
to dead, as my dad
used to say quoting the Public
Service Ad on T V about downed
power lines in the garden of earthly Lost
Almost. Standing up on a bluff
with Lucretius watching the shipwreck
rising up toward us. Here it comes,
my friends. I spit
on poetry with Epicurus, in the hope
of being spit on

in return. I did not mean for this to be a poem
about horseshoe crabs and caged booties, but now
I've watched that 20 seconds on Youtube of feet
twirling slowly over and over, ads for sad
high heels keep showing up in my Face
-book feed. Facebook feed — which at the root
means "nourish
the appearance of the tree," and I could unfold that
one for a while, but I can't stop thinking
of that water
-man in the lo-res
Nature video on my screen, holding
the ancient pre-dinosaur sea spider to his face
saying "See?
They're harmless," as with its claws it
gently probes his cheeks.
                He speaks as a fisherman of the privilege
to return his prey, but in fact
it's not clear how many survive the bleeding
and whether it reduces spawning, and there's a whole
other story here about a bird called the red knot
that seems to be going extinct that makes one of the longest
migrations of any creature, from Tierra del Fuego
to the Arctic, and relies on the greenish strings
of horseshoe crab eggs clotted up on the shore

at just this time for fuel to complete its journey, though I
think the video only features the bird because
horseshoe crabs are not
filled with personality though they do have ten eyes,
and the industry compares the crabs to humans donating
blood but of course
the crabs are forced, and Allison
Argo the filmmaker and narrator intones "There is hardly
a person alive
who does not owe thanks
to the horseshoe crab," but I wonder about all the people
alive on earth who never get treated with a specialty
pharmaceutical through an intravenous drip, and I
remember the trips we took to the Delaware shore without
ever knowing about the tiny horseshoe crab larva hopping
along the sand floor and the many trips I took to the
emergency room for a time and the brownish-purple
IV bruises up my hands and arms, and the horseshoe crab
I saw washed up near the East River once
but didn't think much about it.
          I meant to end this poem with a tight
metaphor about the band Poison from the eighties and how
in retrospect that time with its Cold
War, which literally nourished me, and the men
in makeup on my bedroom wall seems sort of

innocent now and that maybe more insidious forms of
poison have invaded all of us alive on the planet, plant,
human, and animal, and one poison is how we know we
kind of want that
melancholy that lets we who are wealthy in the West
relax into our sadness about the end
of all the stuff we destroyed without knowing or trying, that
clipped and clever cynicism that is a kind of rubbernecking
for we who are
well-off, what the poet and scholar Chris Nealon in his essay
"Infinity for Marxists" calls masochistic species
-shame.
                    So I am failing
at this poem. But maybe failure
is a good place to dwell. Come in
under the shadow of this blood
red rock of the white man's
bank. I can show you how the old
war froze
in place like two gunfighters facing off
forever, hands on holsters, but in this case it's two nations
bristling with missiles still
on hair
-trigger, high alert—set to launch
in fifteen minutes or less at all of them and

all of us. My dears, I can show you fear
in approximately three thousand ninety-seven war
-heads set on missiles, how the practice of bombing
regular people from the air evolved out of World War I
through the British "policing" Iraqis
with bombs in the 1920s, how your shadow falls
behind you and rises to meet you, and you have never
breathed any other air
but this war. The crabs know this too,
in their way, and the zoos with their relic
masticators and the sad
sad sandal stitchers. There is
no other poem but this one, a heap
of broken images where the sun beats
on the dead trees and the dry stone gives
no sound of water, only
failure, from Latin "to trip,
dupe, deceive." Like fake. Is there no
other ending but this one, the fucked up fail
of this war
way of being in the world? How should I know? I'm not
your sibyl
hanging out in a jar. We
all will be the ones
to make that call—we

the targets, we the people
with our fingers on the trigger.
We the late—
the start

IV.

AFTER WE ALL DIED

When was it that everything first died? Someone said when the first atmospheric engine cranked into motion. Someone said when the atomic bomb bloomed over the desert at Trinity Site. But these are only a few of the more recent times when everything died, the latest entrants in a funeral procession winding like water through all of matter. Drip, drip. It disappears into its birthplace, the ocean of dead things, which people think of as time. But people are mistaken about everything. Being mistaken—in other words, having already caused the death of everything—people had to invent a language, with imprecise words—which exist only as imprecision—to try and bridge their confusion: like "thing," and like "time," which are the same, a cutting apart, a gathering.

When was it that everything first died? Maybe it was when humans first made their way to new territory lacking human predators. Like seeds, they planted themselves and sprouted, planted and sprouted, spreading with great increase. Certain males of the species came to see the world as all Apple store or porn portal, a creation dedicated to their desire—a top predator kind of reality, a "what-I-want" lens on the world. It glues its glittering look onto every surface. But doesn't everything look that way? I mean everything that thinks it's alive? The look shines out from each glass-walled eyeball bathed in its device light. Maybe, even, that's what we who have died understand as life. That glitter.

Certain people believed themselves alive. They built arks to save themselves and their favorite TV couples. "Wave goodbye!" they told each other. But like the ship in Coleridge's poem, the boats only filled up with corpses. Corpses armed not with a crossbow but with Apache Longbow Attack Helicopters, MQ-1 Predator drones, Hellfire air-to-ground missiles, M110 sniper rifles, Amphibious Guardian armored security vehicles, Gladiator combat robots, M198 howitzers with a range of twenty miles and GPS aiming, silent submarines circling the ocean packing Trident cruise missiles tipped with multiple nuclear bombs.

Or it happened earlier. The first time a person no longer possessed her own living flesh. The first time one flesh-clad being stripped another down to raw meat to serve desire, the death echo. The word slavery grew from the brutal ground of Christian Europe, but the act itself is much older, seeping like radiation through soil. The flesh understands this in its very sense of itself. The first object was human, and the earth filled up with dead matter.

When was it that everything first died? This obsession with origins betrays my own cataclysmic sincerity. My belief in the delusion that everything could be OK.

O.K.: the only survivor of a slang fad in Boston and New York c. 1838 that abbreviated common phrases with humorous misspellings: K.G. for "know go," and N.C. for "nuff ced." In the case of O.K., the abbreviation is for "oll korrect."

Made popular as an election slogan by the O.K. Club, boosters of Martin Van Buren for president. Woodrow Wilson spelled it o-k-e-h on assumption that it represented the Choctaw word *okeh,* "it is so."

Okay. All right. It is so. The truth is banal: I started out dead, a girl-thing, white to the root, borne up by the race spoils of total war and the blast force of nuclear love. I give birth to this death and I am it, and you, and you, and you—

This is our death. We share it, we who come after the future. With our bodies we nurse our machine that killed us. We give it all of our words. We give it our births to continue, and we who live in privilege: we devour the births out of everything else. The task of such selves is not to live. It is to refuse all the terms of this death into which we were birthed. Maybe then, learning to be dead, something can live.

Notes

I made this

ABOUT RATS:

http://www.arkive.org/brown-rat/rattus-norvegicus/

http://www.ratbehavior.org/rats.html

INVASIVE EARTHWORMS:

Smithsonian Environmental Research Center, "Ecosystems on the Edge," http://eco-systems.serc.si.edu/earthworm-invaders/

Becky Oskin, "Invasive earthworms harm forests near the Great Lakes," *Scientific American,* http://www.scientificamerican.com/article/invasive-earthworms-harm-for-ests-near-great-lakes/

Michael Tennesen, "Invasive Earthworms Denude Forests in U.S. Great Lakes Region," *Scientific American,* http://www.scientificamerican.com/article/invasive-earthworms-denude-forests/

Sentences

Alex Wellerstein's map of U.S. equivalents of Japanese cities firebombed in World War II appeared in *Slate,* March 13, 2014: http://www.slate.com/blogs/the_vault/2014/03/13/map_interactive_visualizing_firebomb_damage_done_to_japan_dur-ing_wwii_through.html

A more in-depth discussion is on Wellerstein's blog: http://blog.nuclearsecrecy.com/2014/03/12/firebombs-usa/

INFORMATION ON THE HISTORY OF AERIAL BOMBING:

A.C. Grayling, *Among the dead cities : the history and moral legacy of the WWII bombing of civilians in Germany and Japan* (New York: Walker & Co., 2006)

Toshiyuki Tanaka and Marilyn Blatt Young, *Bombing civilians: a twentieth-century history* (New York: New Press, 2009)

Sven Lindquist, trans. Linda Haverty Rugg, *A History of Bombing* (New York: New Press, 2003)

Shout at the Devil

Fuck anyone who uses ant poison: Joshua Clover and Juliana Spahr, *Misanthropocene: 24 Theses* (Oakland: Commune Editions, 2014): https://communeditions.files.wordpress.com/2014/08/misanthropocene_web_v2_final.pdf

Cathy Wagner on houses: "'A house we make together that's fragile and strong;': The Site of Voice in Alice Notley's Poetry," unpublished paper presented at Alette in Oakland: A Symposium on the Work of Alice Notley, October 24–26, 2014, hosted by the Bay Area Public School

Cruel optimism: Lauren Berlant, *Cruel Optimism* (Raleigh–Durham: Duke University Press, 2011)

Humans as invasive species: E.O. Wilson, *The Future of Life* (New York: Vintage Books, 2003) 79–102

INFORMATION ABOUT ANTS:

Bert Hölldobler and Edward O. Wilson, *Journey to the Ants: A Story of Scientific Exploration* (Cambridge, MA: Belknap Press, 1994)

Mark W. Moffett, "Supercolonies of billions in an invasive ant: What is a society?" *Behavioral Ecology* (2012) 23 (5): 925–933. Published online: April 20, 2012. doi: 10.1093/beheco/arso43

Julien Foucad, Jérôme Orviel, et al., "Reproductive system, social organization, human disturbance and ecological dominance in native populations of the little fire ant, *Wasmannia auropunctata*," *Molecular Ecology* (2009) 18, 5059–5073

ANTS IN HAWAII:

John Gregg, "Kingdom of the Ants," *Hana Hou!* The Magazine of Hawaiian Airlines, Vol. 17, No. 5 October/November 2014, 131–137

The Hawai'i Ant Lab guidebook "Managing LFA Around Your Home": http://www.littlefireants.com/lfa%20fact%20sheet%202.pdf

INFORMATION ABOUT CANCER AND CHEMICALS:

The two greatest risks for breast cancer: http://www.dslrf.org/breastcancer/content.asp?L2=7&L3=2&SID=232&CID=232&PID=0&CATID=0&d=nn#

Holger M. Koch and Antonia M. Calafat, "Human body burdens of chemicals used in plastic manufacture," *Phil. Trans. R. Soc. B* 2009 364, 2063–2078

Lowell Center for Sustainable Production, "Phthalates and their alternatives: health and environmental concerns," January 2011: http://www.sustainableproduction.org/downloads/PhthalateAlternatives-January2011.pdf

The Centers for Disease Control biomonitoring study results: http://www.cdc.gov/biomonitoring/phthalates_factsheet.html

SUMMARY OF RESEARCH ON PHTHALATES AND BREAST CANCER:

http://www.breastcancerfund.org/clear-science/radiation-chemicals-and-breast-cancer/phthalates.html

INFORMATION ABOUT PHTHALATES AND ANTS:

Alain Lenoir, Virginie Culliver-Holt, et al., "Ant cuticles: a trap for atmospheric phthalate contaminants," *Science of The Total Environment* (Impact Factor: 3.16). 11/2012; 441C:209–212.

David Jolly, "Ant Study Deepens Concerns About Plastic Additives," *New York Times,* January 7, 2013: http://green.blogs.nytimes.com/2013/01/07/ant-study-deepens-con-cern-about-plastic-additives/?_r=0

THE HISTORY AND CURRENT STATE OF CANCER TREATMENT:

Siddhartha Mukherjee, *The Emperor of All Maladies: A Biography of Cancer* (New York: Scribner, 2011)

Reynold Spector, "The War on Cancer, a Progress Report for Skeptics," *Skeptical Inquirer,* Volume 34.1 January/February 2010: http://www.csicop.org/si/show/war_on_cancer_a_progress_report_for_skeptics/

Jake Bernstein, "MIA in the War on Cancer: Where are the low-cost treatments?" *ProPublica,* April 23, 2014: http://www.propublica.org/article/where-are-the-low-cost-cancer-treatments?

Alexander Narayan, "World War Cancer," June 30, 2013: http://www.newyorker.com/tech/elements/world-war-cancer

Anne Boyer quote: "The Sororal Death," *The New Inquiry,* December 2014: http://the-newinquiry.com/essays/the-sororal-death/

ERNEST LAWRENCE:

Gregg Herken, *Brotherhood of the Bomb: the tangled lives and loyalties of Robert Op-penheimer, Ernest Lawrence, and Edward Teller* (New York: Holt, 2003), 10-20, 309

Luis Alvarez, "Berkeley: A Lab Like No Other," *Bulletin of the Atomic Scientists,* April, 1974, 18

Herbert Childs, *An American Genius: The Life of Ernest Orlando Lawrence* (New York: E.P. Dutton & Co., Inc., 1968), 139-175, 192, 220-223, 278

ERNEST LAWRENCE AND URANIUM FOR LITTLE BOY:

Richard Rhodes, *The Making of the Atomic Bomb* (New York: Simon and Schuster, 1986), 601

MICHAEL CAINE'S NEW HOUSE:

Michael Caine, *What's It All About* (New York: Ballantine Books, 1993)

HENRIETTA LACKS AND TISSUE OWNERSHIP LAWS:

Rebecca Skloot, *The Immortal Life of Henrietta Lacks* (New York: Broadway Books, 2010)

Clair Devine, "Tissue Rights and Ownership: Is a Cell line a Research Tool or a Person?" *The Columbia Science and Technology Law Review,* March 9, 2010: http://stlr.org/2010/03/09/tissue-rights-and-ownership-is-a-cell-line-a-research-tool-or-a-person/

Carl Zimmer, "A Family Consents to a Medical Gift, 62 Years Later," *The New York Times,* August 7, 2013: http://www.nytimes.com/2013/08/08/science/after-decades-of-research-henrietta-lacks-family-is-asked-for-consent.html?pagewanted=all&_r=0

ALICE NOTLEY:

Mysteries of Small Houses (New York: Penguin, 1998)

"the kind / Of shaking that keeps you steady" is from an earlier poem, "The Prophet," collected in Graves of Light (Middletown, CT: Wesleyan, 2006).

You were born

THE HORSESHOE CRAB AND THE RED KNOT:

PBS documentary, "Crash: a Tale of Two Species," http://www.pbs.org/wnet/nature/crash-a-tale-of-two-species-introduction/592/

About the Author

ALLISON COBB is the author of *Born2* (Chax Press), *Green-Wood* (Factory School), and *Plastic: an autobiography* (Essay Press). She works for Environmental Defense Fund and lives in Portland, Oregon, where she co-curates the reading, art, and performance series The Switch.

AHSAHTA PRESS

NEW SERIES

AHSAHTA PRESS

SAWTOOTH POETRY PRIZE SERIES

2002: Aaron McCollough, *Welkin* (Brenda Hillman, judge)
2003: Graham Foust, *Leave the Room to Itself* (Joe Wenderoth, judge)
2004: Noah Eli Gordon, *The Area of Sound Called the Subtone* (Claudia Rankine, judge)
2005: Karla Kelsey, *Knowledge, Forms, The Aviary* (Carolyn Forché, judge)
2006: Paige Ackerson-Kiely, *In No One's Land* (D. A. Powell, judge)
2007: Rusty Morrison, *the true keeps calm biding its story* (Peter Gizzi, judge)
2008: Barbara Maloutas, *the whole Marie* (C. D. Wright, judge)
2009: Julie Carr, *100 Notes on Violence* (Rae Armantrout, judge)
2010: James Meetze, *Dayglo* (Terrance Hayes, judge)
2011: Karen Rigby, *Chinoiserie* (Paul Hoover, judge)
2012: T. Zachary Cotler, *Sonnets to the Humans* (Heather McHugh, judge)
2013: David Bartone, *Practice on Mountains* (Dan Beachy-Quick, judge)
2014: Aaron Apps, *Dear Herculine* (Mei-mei Berssenbrugge, judge)
2015: Vincent Toro, *Stereo. Island. Mosaic.* (Ed Roberson, judge)

This book is set in Apollo MT type with Perpetua titles
by Ahsahta Press at Boise State University.
Cover design by Quemadura.
Book design by Janet Holmes.

AHSAHTA PRESS
2016

JANET HOLMES, DIRECTOR

PATRICIA BOWEN, *intern*
SAM CAMPBELL
KATHRYN JENSEN
COLIN JOHNSON
DAN LAU
MATT NAPLES